SPARKLING SYDNEY

Sydney glitters with a seductive charm which captivates the visitor. Set around Port Jackson, one of the world's finest harbours and natural waterways, this multicultural metropolis is a dynamic business capital, a major international travel destination and an exciting place to live. Nearly one-quarter of Australia's population call Sydney home and the city has a vigorous cultural and intellectual energy that fosters innovative music, theatre and art.

Sydneysiders have always known how to enjoy themselves outdoors in their leisure time. The number of sailing boats on the harbour at any time of the year and the large crowds on the beaches on a hot day are a good indication of this. Cosmopolitan and colourful, Sydney has few peers. It is truly one of the world's great cities.

Above: The city, viewed from the north.

Kirribilli, with the city, the Opera House and the Harbour Bridge.

The city skyline glitters at dusk.

The Manly Ferry.

The Opera House and the Harbour Bridge.

3

SYDNEY HARBOUR

Port Jackson is the name given to Sydney's magnificent harbour, one of the finest natural waterways in the world. Large ocean liners call in the summer months when the city is at its best. Dozens of bays and inlets shelter a myriad moored craft which are claimed by their owners for weekend sailing. Some of the city's most exclusive residential development is located on the waterfront bordering the harbour, while Sydney Harbour National Park allows public access to much of the harbour foreshore.

Above: Sailing boats on the harbour.
Below: North Head, at the entrance to Port Jackson.
Left: The Oriana is escorted by a flotilla to its berth at Circular Quay.

SYDNEY HARBOUR BRIDGE

Known affectionately by locals as 'The Coat-hanger', the Sydney Harbour Bridge was considered an engineering feat when it was completed in 1932. Spanning the harbour between Dawes Point at The Rocks and Milsons Point at North Sydney, the highest part of the arch rises 134 metres above the water, the deck is 49 metres wide and the massive steel structure carries 15 000 vehicles per hour during peak hour. As the total volume of daily traffic from this rapidly expanding city is continually increasing, there is now a harbour tunnel which whisks travellers from shore to shore without seeing the light of day.

For the thousands of visitors to Australia from around the world, the bridge is Sydney's welcoming symbol, a familiar landmark in an unfamiliar country. It provides a spectacular centrepiece for the famous harbour, inspiring emotion for all Australians, no matter

The illuminated Sydney Harbour Bridge in the evening light.

West Circular Quay, looking towards the Harbour Bridge.

where they may choose to travel or reside. The south-eastern pylon is open for sightseers, and the bridge itself accessible from The Rocks to pedestrians who wish to walk across the harbour. Breathtaking harbour and city views include the shining shells of the Sydney Opera House. At night, the bridge's lights are elegantly reflected in the water below.

Right: The Royal Botanic Gardens surround Government House, situated behind the Opera House. The Harbour Bridge links the city with North Sydney.

The Opera House and the Harbour Bridge, viewed from Mrs Macquaries Chair.

The evening light on the 'sails' of the Opera House.

The Opera House, and the Oriana berthed at Circular Quay.

A ferry leaving Circular Quay and the Opera House.

THE OPERA HOUSE

Located on Bennelong Point, to the east of Circular Quay, the Sydney Opera House is regarded by many as one of the world's greatest public buildings. It was designed in 1956 by the Danish architect, Joern Utzon, to complement its spectacular harbourside location. The building was not completed until 1973. The Opera House is the venue for live theatre, opera, ballet, modern dance and classical music, although its sightseeing tours are as popular as any of its performances.

An Opera House dining area with a view towards the Harbour Bridge.

A cruise ship moored at the Overseas Passenger Terminal.

CIRCULAR QUAY

Circular Quay, the main terminus within the city for ferries, buses and trains, is the embarkation point for harbour cruises. The sights of Sydney Harbour can also be enjoyed from Sydney's commuter ferries which provide relaxed and unhurried transportation to harbour suburbs such as Manly, Watsons Bay, Mosman, Balmain and Parramatta. A harbourside walkway links The Rocks, the Opera House, the Museum of Modern Art and the Royal Botanic Gardens.

Often moored near Circular Quay is Sydney's HMAV Bounty, an exact-size, fully-rigged replica of Bligh's original vessel built for the movie 'The Bounty'. The vessel is 42 metres long and weighs 400 tonnes. Today, the ship is berthed at historic Campbells Cove at The Rocks. Her concessions to modernity are all below deck and include twin turbo-charged marine diesel engines. HMAV Bounty sails Sydney Harbour every day of the year, giving passengers a taste of eighteenth-century adventure with twentieth-century dining.

HMAV Bounty, moored at Campbells Cove.

Circular Quay, the centre for ferries and overseas passenger liners.

The old Pyrmont Bridge, with the Harbourlink Monorail.

The eastern side of Darling Harbour, looking towards the city.

The National Maritime Museum.

Darling Harbour.

DARLING HARBOUR

Darling Harbour, just to the west of the city centre, is the place to go for shopping and dining. Once railway goods yards, the redevelopment has put new heart into the city as a weekend destination for thousands of people who flock to the exhibition, convention and shopping complexes surrounded by landscaped gardens and walkways. Nearby, the Sydney Aquarium, National Maritime Museum and Powerhouse Museum are major attractions. The old Pyrmont Bridge, now a pedestrian walkway, links the city.

The National Maritime Museum has been established to show how closely Australians are linked to the sea. Its exhibitions explore some of the major influences on Australian life including Aboriginal culture, successive waves of immigration, defence at sea, aquatic sports and seaside recreation. Moored at its wharves, the Museum's 12 historic vessels range from a Vietnamese refugee boat to a naval destroyer.

Right: Sydney Aquarium.

13

The Sydney Tower and the MLC Building.

The Sydney Tower at dusk.

ABOVE SYDNEY

Sydney Tower, the tallest structure in the city, rises above Centrepoint Shopping Centre. The observation deck is an ideal place to get a 360 degree view of the city and suburbs; on a clear day it is possible to see as far as the Blue Mountains in the west. Diners in the three revolving restaurants are slowly and gently treated to the full panorama.

The Monorail runs in a one-way, anti-clockwise loop from Darling Harbour, past the Sydney Convention Centre, Haymarket, Chinatown and Pitt Street back towards Darling Harbour. This sophisticated mode of transport allows passengers to explore the western edge and retail districts travelling in style and comfort above the traffic.

The Harbourlink Monorail, turning into Market Street towards Darling Harbour.

QUEEN VICTORIA BUILDING

Built in 1898 as a produce market, the Queen Victoria Building languished as government offices before restoration in 1986 to one of the finest shopping centres in the world. More than 200 specialty shops occupy the five levels. The building has a variety of artefacts associated with Queen Victoria. The impressive clock, the centrepiece of the building's interior, chimes on the hour. Above the clockface is a revolving historical tableau.

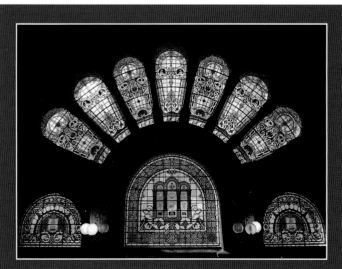

Above: The Queen Victoria Building.
Left: The building's stained glass windows.
Opposite: An interior view of the Queen Victoria Building.

The interior of Saint Mary's Roman Catholic Cathedral.

The portico of the Art Gallery of New South Wales.

HISTORIC SYDNEY

Sydney has many fine old buildings which stand as a testament to days gone by. Designed in the Gothic revival style and started last century, Saint Mary's Cathedral is located just across the road from Hyde Park. Not far away, on Mrs Macquaries Road, the Art Gallery of New South Wales showcases the best of Australian art. The historic old section has been added to and the new wings display a vast selection of art from home and abroad, including excellent examples of Aboriginal art.

Opposite: The impressive Sydney Town Hall, completed in 1889, illuminated at night.

Creperie Stivell, Fiveways, Paddington.

The Tea Centre of Sydney, Glenmore Road, Paddington.

The Country Trader, Glenmore Road, Paddington.

Orson and Blake Collectables, Queen Street, Woollahra.

SHOPPING IN SYDNEY

In Sydney's central business district, pedestrians roam the numerous shopping arcades lining Pitt Street Mall which are linked with large department stores. Nearby, the Queen Victoria Building has been transformed into a prestigious shopping venue to match the classic Victorian-era Strand Arcade between Pitt and George Streets. Retail centres such as Centrepoint, Skygarden and the Glasshouse can also be found in Pitt Street Mall along with hundreds of specialty shops. The inner suburbs of Double Bay, Paddington, Woollahra, Glebe and Newtown have excellent shopping precincts.

Right: Pitt Street Mall runs between Market Street and King Street.
Opposite: The Strand Arcade joins George Street with Pitt Street Mall.

Darling Harbour.

El Alamein Fountain, Kings Cross.

Chinatown mall, Dixon Street.

Sydney Harbour Casino, Pyrmont.

Darlinghurst Road, Kings Cross.

The city, from the Cahill Expressway.

THE CITY AFTER DARK

Sydney comes alive after dark. The cinema district, near the Town Hall on George Street, attracts movie-goers, while Chinatown, centred on Dixon Street at the southern end of the city, is only a short walk from Darling Harbour. This unique part of Sydney has a colourful display of lights and a bustle of evening crowds exploring the myriad shops and restaurants. Prominent among the visitors are those food lovers who come to seek out the specialist regional Chinese cuisines. Kings Cross is the place to go to experience a variety of cosmopolitan restaurants and nightclubs, a hive of activity at all hours of the day and night.

Left: The cinema district on George Street.

Evening view of the city from the old Pyrmont Bridge.

The statue of Apollo atop the Archibald Fountain, Hyde Park.

The Captain Arthur Phillip statue, Royal Botanic Gardens.

THE BOTANIC GARDENS

The harbourside Royal Botanic Gardens are the jewels in the city's crown. Over 30 hectares of magnificent gardens include wide expanses of lawn with colourful beds of exotic and native plants, and two glasshouses containing tropical ferns, orchids and palms.

Above: The Royal Botanic Gardens and the city.
Opposite: The Royal Botanic Gardens looking towards the city.

Anzac War Memorial, Hyde Park.

Taronga's giraffes have one of the world's best views.

TARONGA ZOO

Set in bushland overlooking Sydney Harbour, Taronga Zoological Park has one of the most spectacular settings in the world in which to view the animals. In keeping with a modern zoo's code of presenting exhibits in as natural a setting as possible, staff now care for animals which are well presented and comfortable. Taronga also participates in breeding programs that endeavour to prevent the extinction of endangered species.

Right: Koalas are a popular feature of Taronga Zoo.

The Elephant House, with the city in the background.

Looking toward Cremorne Point and the city from the zoo.

The Lord Nelson Hotel, Sydney's oldest hotel.

Restored Bond Houses at the Rocks which have been converted into restaurants.

The Rocks, at the corner of Argyle and George Streets.

THE ROCKS

A short walk from Circular Quay, The Rocks is the site of the first European settlement in Australia. Convicts from the First Fleet in 1788 cleared the area which gained the name 'The Rocks' because of its sandstone outcrops. Today many of the buildings have been restored along with the original narrow laneways which again ring with the sound of footsteps on cobbled pavements.

Pubs and restaurants mingle with art and craft galleries, boutiques, specialty and gift shops which showcase Australian products such as opals, glassware, sheepskin products and Aboriginal art.

Left: Cadman's Cottage, Sydney's oldest house.

Looking west over Dover Heights and Bondi Beach, towards the city.

SYDNEY BEACHES

Sydney's Beaches are world famous. Bondi Beach, an Australian icon of surf and beach culture, is the most popular suburban beach in Australia. On a summer's day the beach is packed with locals and visitors alike who come to sun themselves and plunge into the cool waters of the Tasman Sea. Shops and cafes line the boulevard that curves around the sandy crescent of the beach.

Somewhat quieter than Bondi, Coogee Beach has a strong following of people who prefer to escape the throng of bathers and sun-seekers. Increasingly, however, as its popularity grows, so do the number of people who wish to enjoy the sun-drenched sand of this picturesque beach so close to the city.

Right: Bondi Beach on a fine day.
Opposite: Looking south over North Steyne and Manly Beaches.

31

The catamaran ferry ride from the city to Manly
is one of the highlights of the Sydney experience.